Seasons

FIRST EDITION
Series Editor Penny Smith; **Art Editor** Leah Germann; **US Editors** Elizabeth Hester, John Searcy;
DTP Designer Almudena Díaz; **Pre-Production Producer** Nadine King; **Producer** Sara Hu;
Picture Research Myriam Megharbi; **Dinosaur Consultant** Dougal Dixon;
Reading Consultant Linda Gambrell, PhD

THIS EDITION
Editorial Management by Oriel Square
Produced for DK by WonderLab Group LLC
Jennifer Emmett, Erica Green, Kate Hale, *Founders*

Editors Grace Hill Smith, Libby Romero, Maya Myers, Michaela Weglinski;
Photography Editors Kelley Miller, Annette Kiesow, Nicole DiMella;
Managing Editor Rachel Houghton; **Designers** Project Design Company;
Researcher Michelle Harris; **Copy Editor** Lori Merritt; **Indexer** Connie Binder; **Proofreader** Larry Shea;
Reading Specialist Dr. Jennifer Albro; **Curriculum Specialist** Elaine Larson

Published in Great Britain by Dorling Kindersley Limited
DK, One Embassy Gardens, 8 Viaduct Gardens, London, SW11 7BW

The authorised representative in the EEA is

Dorling Kindersley Verlag GmbH. Arnulfstr. 124,
80636 Munich, Germany

A catalogue record for this book
is available from the British Library.
ISBN: 978-0-2416-0364-2

Printed and bound in China

The publisher would like to thank the following for their kind permission to reproduce their images:
a=above; c=centre; b=below; l=left; r=right; t=top; b/g=background

123RF.com: Martin Damen 9br, subbotina 6-7, Svetlana Yefimkina 14-15b; **Dreamstime.com:** Agorulko 3cl,
Natalya Aksenova 7br, Mihai Andritoiu 4-5, Vinicius Bacarin 13bl, Chaoticmind 20br, Jolanta Dabrowska 17bc,
Elena Elisseeva / Elenathewise 14-15, Famveldman 20-21, 23bl, Firina 19br, Ivandzyuba 18-19,
Sergey Kichigin / Kichigin 20-21b, Anastasiia Lytvynenko 7bl, Maskarad 16-17b, Ivan Mikhaylov 17br, Alexander Potapov 1b,
Ppy2010ha 16br, Rixie 12br, Scphoto48 12-13, 23cla, Yury Shirokov 11bl, Tatyana Tomsickova 21tr; **Fotolia:** Roman Sigaev 3br,
18br; **Getty Images:** Daniel Truta / EyeEm 10br, Stockbyte / Russell Burden 13br, Stone / Paul Souders 18cb,
The Image Bank / Ariel Skelley 8-9, 23cl; **Getty Images / iStock:** E+ / FatCamera 10-11, 16-17, 23tl, 23clb, jacoblund 22

Cover images: *Front:* **Dreamstime.com:** Tuja

All other images © Dorling Kindersley
For more information see: www.dkimages.com

For the curious
www.dk.com

Seasons

Libby Romero

Come and explore the seasons!

5

It is spring!
The days are warm.
The trees are filling
with green leaves.
Baby animals are born.

spring

Flowers bloom
in the spring.

flowers

The days get hotter.
It is summer.

summer

We go to the beach to cool off.

Animals find ways
to stay cool, too.
They go in the water.
They rest in the shade.

animals

It is autumn.
The days are cool.
The leaves change
colours. Animals
start to collect
and store food.

autumn

pumpkins

We pick pumpkins
in the autumn.

Now, it is winter.
The days are cold.
Snow falls from the sky.
Some animals
go for a long nap.

winter

In the winter,
we play in the snow.

snow

There is a season for everything!

Glossary

autumn
a season when temperatures cool down and leaves change colours

shade
an area sheltered from heat and bright sunlight

spring
a season when temperatures warm up and new growth begins

summer
the hottest season of the year, when many plants grow

winter
the coldest season of the year, with snow falling in some areas

Quiz

Answer the questions to see what you have learnt. Check your answers with an adult.

1. What are the four seasons?

2. In which season are many baby animals born?

3. In which season can you play in the snow?

4. What happens to leaves in the autumn?

5. What is your favorite season? Why?

1. Spring, summer, autumn and winter 2. Spring 3. Winter
4. They change colours 5. Answers will vary